TOWER HAMLETS COLLEGE

043929

Withdrawn

Withdrawn

KT-466-702

b. 99

Withdrawn

Scientists who have changed the world

Thomas A. Edison
by Anna Sproule

OTHER TITLES IN THE SERIES
Alexander Graham Bell by Michael Pollard (1-85015-200-4)
Charles Darwin by Anna Sproule (1-85015-213-6)
Albert Einstein by Fiona Macdonald (1-85015-253-5)
Alexander Fleming by Beverley Birch (1-85015-184-9)
Galileo Galilei by Michael White (1-85015-277-6)
Johann Gutenberg by Michael Pollard (1-85015-255-1)
Guglielmo Marconi by Beverley Birch (1-85015-185-7)
Margaret Mead by Michael Pollard (1-85015-228-4)
Isaac Newton by Michael White (1-85015-243-8)
James Watt by Anna Sproule (1-85015-254-3)
The Wright Brothers by Anna Sproule (1-85015-229-2)

Picture Credits
Ann Ronan: 6, 24, 36, 48; Nick Birch: 12, 13, 26, 29, 34-5, 38, 46 (both); The Bridgeman Art
Library: 12-3, 16, 18, 22, 42, 43; Paul Brierley: 58; British Museum: 4; The Cincinnati Historical
Society: 18; The Edison National Historic Site: 23, 27, 32, 45, 56; Mary Evans: 10, 21, 30-1 (all),
55; Michael Holford: 19; Angelo Hornak: 40; Mansell Collection: 14; The New York Historical
Society: 28; Science Photo Library: 39, 59; Wayland Picture Library: 53; Zefa: 8-9, 17, 50.

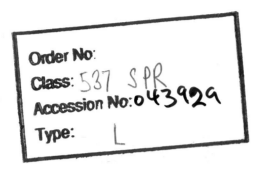

Order No:

Class: 537 SPR

Accession No: 043929

Type: L

Published in Great Britain in 1990
by Exley Publications Ltd,
16 Chalk Hill, Watford,
Herts WD1 4BN, United Kingdom.

Copyright © Exley Publications, 1990
Reprinted 1993.

British Library Cataloguing in Publication Data
Sproule, Anna.
   Thomas A. Edison – (Scientists
   who have changed the world).
   1.   Electrical engineering. Edison,
       Thomas Alva *1847-1931.*
   I.   Title.
   II. Series.
   621.3′092′4

ISBN 1-85015-201-2

All rights reserved. No part of this publication
may be reproduced or transmitted in any form
or by any means, electronic or mechanical,
including photocopy, recording or any
information storage and retrieval system without
permission in writing from the Publisher.

Series editor: Helen Exley.
Picture research: Kate Duffy and
   Caroline Mitchell.
Editing: Samantha Armstrong and
   Margaret Montgomery.
Typeset by Brush Off Studios,
St Albans, Herts AL3 4PH.
Printed and bound in Hungary.

Thomas A. Edison

How electricity was harnessed for domestic use by one of the great inventors of all time

Anna Sproule

THE LIBRARY
TOWER HAMLETS COLLEGE
POPLAR HIGH STREET
LONDON E14 0AF
Tel: 071-538 5888

Rafael
N.Y. 1926

The sound of the past

The machine talked. All but one of the men that stood round it that December evening in 1877 felt the hair stirring on the backs of their necks. Outside the laboratory, the fields and lanes of the New Jersey landscape were gripped tight by the coming winter. It wasn't the cold, though, that made the lab workers shiver.

No human being had ever heard a noise like the one that the little machine produced. The men were listening to the sound of someone talking: not talking then and there, but talking in the past. They were hearing the first recording of a voice ever made.

To be sure, the first words retrieved from the past did not quite match the importance of the moment. Crackling but distinct, the machine recited a fragment of nursery lore:

"Mary had a little lamb,
  Its fleece was white as snow,
  And everywhere that Mary went
  The lamb was sure to go . . ."

But, for all the listeners cared, it could have been reciting a railway timetable. There was a stunned silence. "God in Heaven," breathed John Kreusi, the bushy-bearded Swiss watchmaker who had made the machine's bright brass cylinder and the handle that turned it. Then, abruptly, the spell broke. The men laughed, slapped each other's backs and shouted with jubilation.

The man who made things work, with (below) his most famous invention – the talking machine that, on a winter evening in 1877, first recaptured the sound of the past. In this symbolic portrait by a South American artist, Thomas A. Edison has been given electric light bulbs for ears. In fact, the man who brought sound recording into the world had been deaf from childhood.

5

The wonders of recorded sound. From children to little old ladies, people would line up to hear the newly-invented phonograph. This sketch was made at an exhibition in Paris, where the talking machine's inventor was known as "the astonishing Edison". At home in the United States, he had an even more impressive nickname – people called him "the Wizard".

The man who could not hear

The only person who didn't join in was the machine's inventor: the lab's owner and boss, known by his staff as the "Old Man". Deaf from boyhood, he heard only silence. Ah well, he hadn't expected much from this latest idea anyway. But, even if he could hear nothing, what about the evidence of his eyes? There were the rest of the crew, laughing and whooping loud enough to bring the roof down. Had something happened after all?

Pushing his tousled hair back off his forehead, the inventor bent over the table, re-adjusted the machine, and turned the handle again. Obediently, the cylinder with its shining tinfoil cover turned too, moving along the rod on which it was mounted. As it went along, it moved under a blunt needle, mounted at the end of a short, stubby tube. And, from the other end of the tube, there came again the familiar words, "Mary had a little lamb . . ."

Crackling and scratchy though the sound was, this time the "Old Man" managed to hear it. It was his own voice, captured a few minutes before when he had recited the nursery rhyme. Another needle, mounted on the far side of the cylinder, had trans-formed the sound into a groove scratched in the tinfoil, winding round and round the cylinder from one end to another. As the cylinder turned, the playing needle was now running over the groove its twin had scratched. And, as it ran, it played the rhyme back to the exulting audience. It was all so simple; it was shattering. Awed, the inventor stared at his invention.

With Mary's little lamb, the world's sound record-ing industry had been born. Called the phonograph, or "sound writer", the machine with the revolving cylinder was the ancestor of both the gramophone and today's record player. Its creator was also the world's first recording artist. He was Thomas Alva Edison, aged thirty: a rumpled, self-taught inven-tor, who still spoke with the nasal twang of the American Midwest where he had been born.

Creating a new world

Thomas A. Edison was perhaps one of the greatest inventors that have ever lived. He did not merely change the world he was living in. His inventions helped bring a totally different world into exist-ence: the one we are living in today. The phono-graph was only one of them. Another was the first successful movie camera, along with the equipment for viewing the films it took. Edison also trans-formed the early telephone invented by Alexander Graham Bell into something that would work much better. He did the same with the typewriter. He worked on projects as varied as vacuum-packed food, an X-ray machine, and a system of building

"We are inclined to regard him as one of the wonders of the world."
"Scientific American", commenting on Edison and the phonograph, 1878.

"Edison succeeded, where others failed or never tried, because it was his nature to dare.... He was an eternal optimist who would not let himself or others consider the possibility of failure."
Robert Conot, from "A Streak of Luck".

The world that Thomas Edison helped to create: the skyline of present-day New York, lit by its millions of sparkling lights. The offices where they turn night into day could not function without electricity and the skyscrapers themselves could never have been built. Without electrical power, industry would still be in the steam age, and countless innovations that we take for granted today could never have come into existence.

houses cheaply out of concrete. Above all, he helped to bring civilization out of the Age of Steam and into the Age of Electricity.

The key with which he unlocked the door to the modern world was a tiny one. If you look at an electric light bulb, you are looking at a reminder of his greatest achievement. He created the thread-like filament that glows when the light is turned on. Other inventors were working on the same thing and, in Britain, the great scientist, Joseph Swan, made his breakthrough at almost the same time that Edison did. But Edison took his own work much, much further.

Having made the key to the future, Edison made the door as well. Without electricity, the light bulb was no use. Without a system to bring electric power to everyone who wanted it, he'd have been wasting his time. So he created the system too: a complete

system, from the great dynamos that produced the electric power right down to the light bulbs' sockets.

Proving them wrong

Plenty of people had scoffed at Edison and his ideas. Scientists said they couldn't be done. What did a hick from the sticks of the Midwest know about the subtle new science of electricity? Edison himself scoffed back. What was the use, he asked, of all that pencil-and-paper business? It was the results that mattered. And there was only one way of getting them: hours, days, weeks and even years spent at the laboratory bench, trying one experiment after another until, in the end, something worked.

In spite of his crude knowledge, Edison made things work. Looking back, people now believe

that this ignorance actually *helped* him to make things work. The self-taught inventor, who left school when he was only twelve, didn't know that something was theoretically impossible. He just leapt in and, time and time again, proved the theorists wrong.

Will he live?

The scientists of the United States and Europe weren't the first people to shake their heads over the doings of Thomas A. Edison. He had been causing head-shaking from the day he was born, in the snow-swept town of Milan, Ohio, near Lake Erie. His parents were Canadians. His father owned a timber business. His mother, then nearly forty, had already had six children, and seen three die. When, before dawn on February 11, 1847, Nancy Edison's seventh baby was born, she feared that he might die too. He was so weak, and his head was so big. But, in spite of Nancy's fears, the newest Edison survived. His parents gave him the family name of Thomas. At the same time, his father, Sam, decided to remember a business friend by giving baby Tom the middle name of Alva. Shortened to "Al", it was the name the baby grew up with.

Al asks why

It was a lonely business, being Al. He had no playmates at home; his brother and two sisters were much older than him.

But he soon discovered that there was plenty to play with. The little town was full of excitements. There was his father's timber yard, with its nose-tingling smells. There was the canal, where Al once nearly drowned. There was the big flour mill, huffing and puffing with steam-driven machinery. Even better, there was the mill's owner, who was building a balloon to take people into the air!

Full of curiosity, Al had his nose into everything going on. He'd watch, wonder and plague people with questions. Then, armed with the answers, he'd test his new-found knowledge for himself. Why, he

Opposite: Just a hick from the sticks? Radiating confidence, Edison lounges against a bench in the laboratory he built for himself in the New Jersey countryside. When it came to finding backers for his ventures, his belief in himself and his inventions far outweighed his lack of academic background. Along with his amazing energy, his never-failing enthusiasm was a major cause of his success.

11

Al Edison, aged fourteen. By this time, he had left school and was earning his living as a newspaper boy on the local railway from Port Huron to Detroit.

once asked his mother, does a goose sit on her eggs? His mother told him. So, why did the goose want to keep her eggs warm? His mother told him that too. Very thoughtful, Al vanished for the afternoon. When, at last, his father found him, he was asleep in a nest of straw in a next-door barn. Underneath him, in a mass of cracked shells and leaking yolks, was a big collection of fresh farmyard eggs.

Geese, Al realized, could hatch eggs. But, for some reason, people couldn't.

Bottom of the class

Al loved learning things for himself like this. But school was different. Al went to school when he was eight, not long after his family had moved house to Port Huron, on another of the Great Lakes. Imprisoned every day in the one-room classroom, he felt utterly lost.

Like most teachers of the time, the schoolmaster

believed in beating knowledge into his pupils. Al was frightened of the cane, but he still couldn't learn the great lists of facts the teacher told him to. His habit of asking questions just made the teacher even more angry.

Al sank to the bottom of the class and stayed there for three months. Then he heard the schoolmaster talking about him; there was something wrong with young Edison, the man said. He was "addled". Al knew what that meant: addled eggs were bad ones, rotten ones. In a rage, he rushed out of the schoolroom and refused to go back.

Learning at home

At home, his mother, Nancy, took his side in the battle. For a while, Al went to other schools – off and on. Most of the time, his mother taught him herself. Or rather, she let him run his own education. With her encouragement, he read and read:

Above left: Linked to the outside world by both its railway and its wagon-teams, this small town in the American Midwest was sketched around the time that Edison himself still lived in one. Covered wagons heading west were a frequent sight in the inventor's birthplace of Milan, Ohio.

Above right: The room where, on a snowy night in February 1847, Thomas Alva Edison was born. Edison's mother played an important part in helping Al's abilities to emerge. A former teacher herself, she built up his confidence and let him learn at his own pace.

Shakespeare, history books, the Bible. One day, when he was nine, she gave him his first book on science. Called the *"School of Natural Philosophy"*, it gave readers simple experiments they could carry out at home. From that moment, Al's life was transformed.

Fascinated, he read the book from cover to cover and did all the experiments. Then he made up his own. He bought chemicals, scrounged oddments, like wire, and set up a laboratory in his bedroom. One of his experiments involved the rubbing together of the fur of two big cats, whose tails he had attached to wires ... in an attempt to create static electricity; the only result was that he was scratched and clawed!

In another of his earliest experiments he gave a friend a large quantity of "Seidlitz" powder to take. He was hoping that the gas which the powder generated inside the boy might send him flying through the air just like a balloon when it is filled with volatile air.

His mother gave him her blessing – up to a point. Angry over her wrecked furniture, she insisted that the lab should be taken down to the cellar. Thuds and explosions sometimes shook the house. They startled Al's father who, like the schoolmaster, was always ready to use the cane on his odd, headstrong son. But Nancy would calm Sam down. Al, she'd say, knew quite well what he was doing.

As a boy, Edison watched a hot-air balloon like this one being built by Milan's miller, Sam Winchester. Without knowing it, Winchester taught Al a lot about scientific persistence. The miller took years to build a balloon that would actually fly. Sadly, it vanished with its builder on its first flight – and was never seen again!

The newsboy

For the people of Port Huron, 1859 was an important year. That was when the railway came, linking the lakeside town with the bustling city of Detroit.

Before the railway came North America was full of small isolated towns with little or no contact between them. The only means of transport for both goods and people was by horse-drawn carriage – across thousands of miles of wild territory.

Now Port Huron was really going somewhere. Twelve-year-old Al decided to go with it.

He had several reasons. His family, for a start, was short of money. He himself always needed more cash for his expensive hobby in the cellar. And school – when he went to it – was as useless as ever. In fact, it was worse. Sometimes, Al couldn't hear what the teacher said. Why didn't she speak louder? Bored and restless, he was always getting into trouble. It was time to be moving on.

With his father's help, Al got a job. He became a newsboy on the train that went to and fro on the Port Huron-Detroit line. As well as newspapers, he sold sweets and refreshments. Laden with his basket of wares, he would walk up and down between the seats, shouting out, "Peanuts, popcorn, chewing gum, candy!"

Trains and chemicals

Al's day started at dawn, when he got up to catch the morning train south to Detroit. The evening train back got to Port Huron at half past nine. Then the newsboy still had to get home, in a horse-drawn cart he drove himself.

He was gloriously happy. He was now making money. If he wanted, he could spend his spare time at the Detroit Free Library, reading for hours. As for his precious hobby, he brought it with him. The guard let him keep his sweets and papers in an empty luggage van. Gradually, Al installed his chemicals and equipment there too. All went well until, one day, he set fire to the carriage. The guard, who got burned in the conflagration, threw the whole mobile laboratory out onto the track.

A place called Shiloh

Al was still working the Detroit-Port Huron train when, in 1861, the American Civil War broke out. For four years the northern and southern states fought each other over issues such as the abolition of slavery. Over a million men were killed or wounded. One dreadful battle followed another, and the public became desperate for news. But it was difficult for Al to estimate how many papers he would sell. If he had too few, he might lose business; if he had too many, he might have copies left unsold. To get around this problem, Al made

"The happiest time in my life was when I was twelve years old. I was just old enough to have a good time in the world, but not old enough to understand any of its troubles."
Thomas Edison in 1930, recalling his boyhood.

"I built a telegraph wire between our houses.... The wire was that used for suspending stove pipes, the insulators were small bottles pegged on ten-penny nails driven into the trees. It worked fine."
Thomas Edison, recalling his home-made telegraph system.

15

sure he saw a proof copy of the main story in each day's paper. This way he could be sure he had plenty of stock on days when the news was important.

On April 6, 1862, news came to the Detroit newspaper office of a battle in a place called Shiloh. Over twenty thousand men were lying dead or injured. For anyone in the newspaper business, this was a very big story indeed. If only, thought paperboy Al, the news of Shiloh could be sent to all the towns along the Detroit-Port Huron line. Everyone would want to read about it. He'd sell hundreds of papers at every railway station. Then, suddenly, he realized that he could make it happen. Quick as a flash he could send a message by electricity.

He would use the telegraph.

The electric telegraph

Sending messages over long distances was the main job for which electricity was then used and for most people in 1862, electricity and the telegraph – or

A river battle in the American Civil War between the states of the North and those of the South. The bombardment shown here was kept up for over three weeks by the North's ships. It only ended when the southerners surrendered their fortress on the island in the distance. The war caused dreadful suffering on both sides, and some of the conflicts involved have still not been settled.

"long-distance writer" – meant the same thing. Before the telegraph the only means of communication over long distances was by using signalling methods such as semaphore but these generally only worked if the signallers were close enough to see each other. The electric telegraph could carry messages much further than that.

The special piece of equipment that made the telegraph work was also new. Called an electromagnet, it had been invented forty years before, in the 1820s. It was a piece of metal with a length of wire coiled around it. When an electric current was sent along the wire, the metal became a magnet, and attracted iron. The effect only lasted as long as the current was flowing through the coil. As soon as it stopped, the magnet turned back into an ordinary piece of metal again.

To work the telegraph, the operator at one end of the line tapped a lever. This set an electric current flowing down the wire for a moment. At the other end, the current turned a piece of

Supper, western-style – here served to members of a survey team mapping out the geography of Wyoming. Very soon, Edison's America was also to become the America of the Wild West, with its cowboys, shoot-outs and huge distances between towns. Even in the East, the distances between towns could be big enough and one of the things that helped to hold the vast country together was the telegraph.

metal into an electromagnet, which attracted an iron lever to it. This second lever had a pencil fixed to it. When the current activated the electromagnet, the second lever was attracted to it causing the pencil on the lever to make a mark on a roll of paper as it moved.

Short taps, long taps

The man who designed the American telegraph, an artist named Samuel Morse, also invented a code the pencil could write down. A short tap on the key made the pencil at the other end write a dot. A firmer, longer tap made the pencil write a dash. Each letter of the alphabet was given its own dot-and-dash code. Operators at the other end of the wire would then read the rows of dots and dashes and turn them back into ordinary writing.

It was a simple system and, by Al Edison's time, it was becoming even simpler. Operators could now recognize each letter by the pattern of short and long clicks it made. So they had begun to de-code messages straight off the machine. Al could do the same himself, very slowly. The year before, he'd set up a home-made telegraph between his home and that of a friend, powering it with batteries from his cellar store. But now, on the day of the battle of Shiloh, he needed the help of a "professional", the telegraph operator at Detroit Station.

Opposite top: Riding without charge on puffing, smoke-trailing trains like this one, young Edison would spend several years of his life drifting from town to town as a "tramp" telegrapher. If he couldn't get a free railway pass, he walked.

Opposite bottom: A place called Shiloh. The battle of Shiloh, fought on April 6 and 7, 1862, was one of the bloodiest battles of the American Civil War. Here, northern troops doggedly defend a section of their battle line called the "Hornet's Nest". Although the southerners were beaten, the northerners did not think of Shiloh as a victory: they gained very little, and lost more soldiers than the southerners did.

Left: A telegraph "sounder" – or receiver – of Edison's time, which gave out staccato clicks in the "dot-and-dash" Morse code. In spite of his deafness, Edison became an expert at recording even the fastest messages sent over the telegraph wires. He never became as skilled in transmitting, mainly because he was clumsy with his hands.

Read all about it!

Racing down there, Al burst in and begged the startled man to contact all the stations down the line, telling them that a great battle had taken place. In return, the newsboy promised rashly, he'd give the operator a free subscription to a magazine – no, *two* magazines – and a free newspaper, all for six months. No sooner had the telegraph operator agreed than Al was off again, back to the newspaper offices.

Usually, he only bought a hundred papers for selling on to his customers. This time he asked for 1500! It was a huge risk; even though he couldn't pay for them right then, he knew he would have to later. If he didn't sell the 1400 extra copies.... As the train rumbled out of Detroit, he could scarcely wait to find out if the telegrapher had kept his word.

He had. Normally, Al only sold two papers at the first station on the line. This time, he sold two hundred. At the next, he sold three hundred – and put the price up. By the time he reached Port Huron, the price had reached a quarter of a dollar, and was still rising. By the end of the day, his sales showed a magnificent profit.

It was the first time in Al's life that electricity had made him rich. It would not be the last.

Working on the telegraph

No one was surprised when, aged sixteen, Al became a telegraph operator himself. Since shortly after Shiloh, he had been studying telegraphy with an operator on his train route, using the transmitting key, and working up his receiving speeds. His first job was in the telegraph office of his home town. Not many messages came to Port Huron, so there was plenty of time to experiment with the batteries, wires and other electrical equipment lying around. Al couldn't have been happier. It was as good as his old lab on the train. And it all ended in much the same way, for one of his experiments almost blew the office up. Time to move on again!

For the next five years, the young man wandered

Telegraphy was not the only method of long-distance communication used by Americans in the late 1800s. This engraving shows an alternative – and much older – system for sending signals at work. Like the telegraph, it had obvious uses in warfare. The United States' Indian Wars lasted until 1880, when the Indians' final defeat opened the West up to the invaders.

the United States and the nearby border areas of Canada, working as a "tramp" telegrapher. He would stay in a job a while, then get tired of it – or be sacked – and move on to another one. Cheeky and unreliable, Al was sacked quite often.

However, his skills as a telegraph receiver grew all the time. But so did the hearing troubles that had bothered him from his schooldays. Still in his teens, he was becoming deaf. Oddly enough, his deafness actually helped him in his work. The sharp clicking of the telegraph machine came clearly through the muzziness that filled his ears. But he was protected from all the ordinary office noises that would have distracted him.

Al was good at his work, and he knew it. So he cut corners, played jokes, made up messages and, all the time, went on with his experiments – within working hours as well as out of them.

"Edison would come strolling in and blandly ask some of us to lend him half a dollar with which to get his supper. When reminded he had received half a month's salary that day he would smile, and taking a brown, paper-covered parcel from under his arm, he would display a Ruhmkorff coil, an expensive set of helices or something equally useless...."

Telegrapher Walter Phillips, who worked with Edison.

Experiments – and the sack

His bosses liked Al's scientific tinkering even less than they liked his cockiness. They were plagued by it from the start. Al's first job after Port Huron took him to Stratford, Ontario, where he worked

Telegraph operators at work, sending messages (a transmitting key is being used on the left) and receiving them. By the time this sketch was made, Edison had succeeded in turning one of his earliest dreams into reality. In the 1870s, he would produce a "multiplex" system that allowed several messages to travel over a wire at the same time. In this picture, four messages are passing along the same wire.

21

the night shift. (He always preferred working nights, since it left the days free for science.) To show they were awake, night-workers were meant to send a special signal to headquarters every so often. This was no good to Al. He had better things to do – like sleeping! So he rigged up a clockwork timer that, every hour, sent the signal down the wire automatically!

One place sacked him because he spilt a jar of acid he'd been experimenting with. The acid burnt its way through the floor, the ceiling below, and the carpet of the room downstairs. Another telegraph office sacked him much more unfairly. In Memphis, Tennessee, he managed to set up a direct link between New York and New Orleans. To do this difficult job, he used another telegraph gadget he'd invented, a repeater. His boss was angry, as he'd been trying to set up the link himself. He did not appreciate being shown up by bumptious young Al. So the inventor was thrown out again, without pay.

The noisy, bustling cities of the United States, with their handsome buildings and their gaslit streets, must have seemed like another world to Edison, with his small-town background. Scenes like this one teemed with opportunities. Although Edison did not yet recognize it, the gas street lamps offered him the biggest opportunity of all!

Boston, the heart of science

Al, now twenty-one, drifted on from job to job. In 1868 – hungry, shabby and broke – he ended up in Boston, where he signed on with the big Western Union Telegraph Company. Then, with his job safe, he plunged into the swirl of the city's scientific life.

Boston was at the heart of everything that was happening in American science. It was where the best technicians in the country had their workshops and businesses. Their needs were met by other shops, selling anything a scientist could want: books, chemicals, equipment. In one of these shops, Al happily spent his pay on the works of the great British scientist, Michael Faraday, the father of electrical engineering. In others, like Charles Williams' electrical shop on Court Street, he made some friends. Inventors like himself had formed an unofficial club there. He moved his lab gear into Williams' factory, and worked like one possessed.

Mr. Edison – inventor

Late in 1868, Al played a prank on his Western Union bosses. To keep his speed up, he had transcribed messages in writing so tiny that readers needed a magnifying glass. When he was told to write properly, he switched over to handwriting a foot high. He was promptly demoted – and walked out. In December, a small paragraph in his trade journal said he could be contacted at Williams' factory. In January 1869, it was followed by another one: "T.A. Edison," it announced proudly, "has resigned his situation in the Western Union office, Boston, and will devote his time to bringing out inventions."

He was no longer Al, the drifter from somewhere out West. He was young Mr. Edison, inventor.

Risks and failures

The young inventor soon found out that his new career was much more demanding than his old one. It was also very much riskier. Unless he sold his inventions, he would earn nothing. He would earn

Lean, hungry, and always hard-up: Al Edison as a young man. He spent most of his telegrapher's wages on scientific apparatus, so he always lived in the cheapest lodging-houses he could find. In Cincinnati, his lodgings were full of rats. To get rid of them, he built an electrical rat-trap: one of his very first inventions.

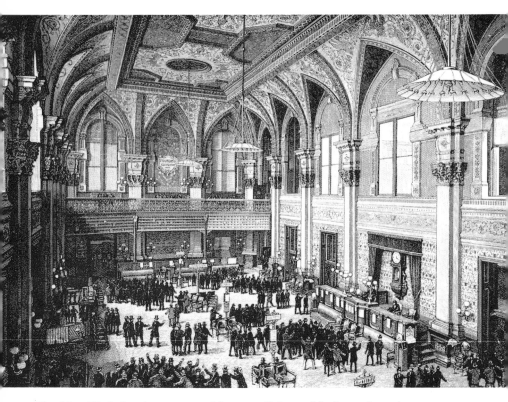

The New York Stock Exchange, scene of minute-to-minute changes in the prices of stocks and gold. Until the mid-1860s, news of these changes was carried to the Wall Street businessmen in their offices by messenger boys. Then, in 1865, a gold dealer named Dr. Laws had the idea of using telegraph apparatus for sending out the changing gold prices. The idea would make him his fortune – and lay the foundations of Edison's, as well.

nothing *until* he sold them but there was a way round that. He would find people to back him, to put money into his projects.

Edison had discovered that he was a born salesman while he was still at Western Union. All his life, he brimmed with confidence and enthusiasm about the inventions he planned, and this enthusiasm was catching. He was good company, too, and always ready with a funny story. Being self-employed made him work even harder at finding Bostonians with money, and here he succeeded.

But he hit a different snag, a much bigger one.

When put to the test, his lovingly-built inventions actually had to work! Some did. And some didn't. The successes included a "stock ticker", a telegraph-type machine used by businesses to keep track of the price of stocks, shares and gold. The machine printed the information sent down its wires on a long ribbon of "ticker tape". Edison built an improved version, and patented it.

Top of the failures was the double-message tele-graph system, or duplex, that Edison set up be-tween New York and Rochester, four hundred miles away on Lake Ontario. To test it, the inventor stationed himself at Rochester. Again and again, he tried to get sense out of distant New York. But nothing worked.

His duplex was useless; his reputation was in ruins. Worse, he had run out of money. It was time to be moving on again. Eighteen months after arriv-ing half-starved and penniless in Boston, Edison turned up in New York. He was just as broke as he'd been eighteen months before – and even hungrier.

Hungry in New York

Now what? The first thing was food. Ravenously, Edison stared at the food stalls, then in the windows of the shops. One of them sold tea; inside, Edison could see a customer being given a free sample. Struck by an idea, the young man marched in and got a sample for himself. Then he found an eating-house, and bartered his tea for a meal. The packet bought one cup of coffee and one apple dumpling. Feeling better, Edison then started tramping the streets in search of friends who could help him.

He found two. The first, another out-of-work telegrapher, lent him a dollar. The second was a top telegraph engineer named Franklin L. Pope. Pope worked at New York's Gold Indicator Com-pany, founded not long before by gold dealer Dr. S.S. Laws. It had been Dr. Laws who had in-vented the very earliest version of the stock ticker. This, the gold indicator itself, showed the changing prices at which gold was being bought and sold. These prices were telegraphed to offices that hired the service.

Naturally, Pope knew of Edison's own stock ticker. Edison, he realized, was just the sort of man the company needed; too bad there were no jobs going right then in its Wall Street headquarters in New York. But the older man had an idea. While he was looking for work, why didn't Edison move

"The telegraph was still the most important application of electricity then [1860s] developed. Its value had been highlighted by the Civil War.... Yet the telegraph was only an augury of things to come. In the busy workrooms of the men who made and repaired telegraph instruments there was already a burning belief that the new system could be developed, adapted, improved and expanded to carry out many tasks other than sending messages across hundreds of miles with a speed that would have been inconceivable only a generation previously."

Ronald W. Clark, from "Edison: the man who made the future".

"Mr Edison had his desk in one corner and after completing an invention he would jump up and do a kind of Zulu war dance. He would swear something awful. We would crowd round him and he would show us the new invention and explain it to the pattern maker and tell us what to do about it."

A Newark worker, remembering his boss.

A stock-ticker from the Newark factory: Edison's own version of the telegraphic machine that printed out the news of changing stock prices. As the "Edison Universal Stock Printer", it was used all over the western world.

into the company building anyway? He could sleep in the cellar, use Pope's office in the day, and get to know how the Indicator's transmitter worked. Edison didn't need asking twice. He moved in.

Edison fixes it

So far, so good; he had a roof over his head, and a dollar to live off. But there was even better to come. Edison had been camping out at Wall Street for only a few days when, suddenly, the office was plunged into chaos. The master machine, on which hundreds of New York businesses depended for their information on gold prices, came to a grinding, crunching halt. It had broken down.

Within minutes, the office was full of messengers from other offices, all desperate to know what was happening. Pope and Dr. Laws were desperate as well. Pope couldn't find what was wrong. Laws, who saw his business collapsing as he watched, began to shout and storm. The engineer and his boss were raving at each other when they heard someone say he thought he could fix it.

It was Edison. During the turmoil, he had looked the transmitter over and noticed a broken spring that had jammed the machine's workings. Within two hours, he'd put it right. Wall Street could run smoothly again, and Dr. Laws' business was saved. By the end of the next day, Edison had a job – helping Pope.

Naming his price

From then on, Edison's fortunes in New York were made. At first, he worked for Laws. Later, he set up his own engineering business. His reputation grew, and he was hired by Western Union to sort out problems they were having with their equipment. He did it so well that the telegraph company decided to buy his improvements outright.

Edison was called into the boss's offices, and asked to name his price. When the young inventor hesitated – he wanted $5,000 but didn't dare ask for it – the boss made an offer himself. How about

$40,000? "This caused me to come as near fainting as I ever got," was how Edison remembered the moment.

The Newark works

Forty thousand dollars! It was a fortune. Edison wasted no time in investing it in a big new workshop. He moved out of New York into nearby New Jersey, and set up his headquarters at a factory in Newark, with space for a hundred-and-fifty workers.

At Newark, the tramp telegrapher became a boss himself, running a factory that made stock-tickers and other telegraphic equipment. But he was still an inventor. He improved a newly-invented system for sending telegraph messages automatically, at a much faster rate than human operators could achieve. He went back to his work on sending more than one message along a single wire.

The Newark team included several men who would play an important part in the inventor's life. John Kreusi was one; Charles Batchelor, an engineer from Britain, was another. Under Edison's rule, this inner team found themselves working day and night – jollied, goaded, instructed and inspired. Totally trusting their fiery "Old Man" and his convictions, they would have sold their souls for him.

In 1871, another important person came into Edison's life. He fell in love with one of his own workers. Her name was Mary Stilwell. She was beautiful, shy and deeply in awe of her brilliant boss and admirer.

Edison, aged twenty-four, married Mary on Christmas Day that year and – so one story says – went straight back to his factory on his wedding day and stayed there till midnight!

Mr. Bell's telephone

In 1876, two things happened that had important consequences for Edison's Newark team. The first was that their employer decided to move out of town. He already had a thriving engineering works, but he wanted something more. He wanted to set up a place that produced, not just goods, but ideas

Aged sixteen, and already married: Edison's first wife, Mary. She worshipped her gifted husband. He loved her for her beauty, her sweetness – and her total docility. At Menlo Park, the couple lived close to the laboratory. But Edison often went for days without seeing much of his wife. He worked in the lab by night, and slept there by day. Later, his three children by Mary would recall that he hardly ever saw them either.

– an "inventions factory". He bought land in a village twelve miles away, called Menlo Park, and started to have a laboratory built there.

The other big event of the year affected many more people than Edison's team. It took place in Boston, where a Scotsman named Alexander Graham Bell was working on an amazing new version of the telegraph. He was trying to use electricity to transmit not a message in dot-and-dash Morse, but the sound of the human voice itself. In 1876, he succeeded. The telephone had been born.

Immediately, everyone in the world of long-distance communications wanted to know more. What was this new gadget? How did it work? Most important of all, would there be money in it? It looked as though there might be. The problem was that the new invention, astounding though it was, needed improvements. The transmitter doubled as the receiver, so users were constantly juggling the equipment between mouth and ear. Its sound was faint and, at first, the signal did not carry for distances of more than a few miles. Western Union hired Edison to see if he could make the necessary improvements.

Downtown New York, as Edison had known it: thrusting, hustling, and completely committed to the goal of making money. It was a perfect place for the inventor, whose aim was always to make things that would sell. When he left for New Jersey and rural Menlo Park, he took New York's hustle with him.

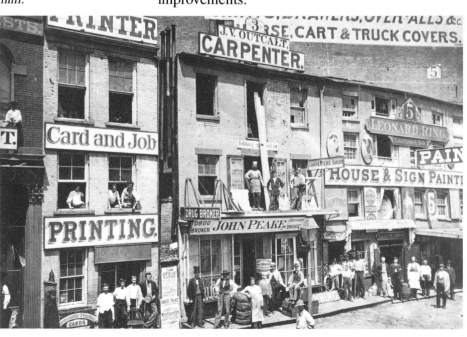

Making electricity ...

At the core of the new telephone invention lay the tried-and-true device of a coil of wire surrounding an iron bar, the electromagnet. But this was not quite like the one used for the telegraph, *for the bar in the telephone was a magnet already.* The coil was different too – it was not linked to a source of electric current. Instead, the device would, under certain conditions, itself produce electricity.

The telephone exploited a discovery made earlier that century by Michael Faraday. Faraday knew that, by activating an electromagnet, electricity could make things move. Turning this idea inside out, he linked movement with a magnet to create electricity. He showed that, if the magnet was moved in and out of the coil, it "induced" an electric current in the wire. The same thing happened if the coil was moved to and fro instead. The movement could be supplied by a variety of things; in the telephone, it was supplied by the human voice.

... and making sound

All the sounds we hear are produced by objects vibrating. Moving though the air, the sounds reach the part of our ears called the ear drum. This, like the surface of a real drum, is made of a thin piece of material called a membrane. When the membrane is hit by the sound waves caused by the distant vibrations, it vibrates too. The inner part of the ear turns these vibrations into electrical signals, and our brains translate the signals into messages we can "hear" and understand.

Bell had built a machine that, in a simple way, duplicated the human ear. When someone spoke into his telephone, the sound of the speaker's voice caused vibrations in a replica ear drum: a flat, thin disk of iron called a diaphragm, mounted inside the telephone. Next to it was the magnet, inside its coil. The movements of the vibrating disk transferred themselves to this, and induced small amounts of electric current. Because the original sounds varied in strength and pattern, the amounts of current varied too.

An early telephone, as created by Alexander Graham Bell. Edison would soon improve it by revolutionizing its method of transmitting an electrical signal. Bell also had a connection with deafness, though a more remote one than Edison had. Bell came to his work on the production of the human voice through his experiences as a teacher of the deaf.

Before the telegraph breakthrough long-distance communication was almost impossible. Smoke signals and carrier pigeons were early methods used to try to overcome the problem.

Another method was semaphore (third picture on the right), in which each letter is shown by a different arm or flag movement. Each person had to be within eyesight of the other to exchange information.

It was not until the telegraph was perfected that a message could be received quickly and clearly by a person who could not actually see the sender.

The constantly varying current passed down the wire to the telephone's receiving end. Here, the electrical variations turned themselves back into vibrations in another diaphragm: vibrations that were twins to the original ones made by the speaker's voice. And it was this voice – distorted and faint, but still this voice – that the listener heard.

Currents and carbon

Edison tackled the problems set by Bell's equipment on several different fronts. He decided to separate the transmitter part of the machine from the receiving one. He also knew that a different method of transmission was needed altogether: one which produced a stronger, clearer signal. The power needed boosting as well.

For the new transmitter, Edison decided to do without magnets completely. Instead, he planned to use another way of making electrical currents vary. To do it, he would use the electrical principle of resistance.

Resistance is the word we use for the extent to which something hinders the flow of electricity. We

could call it the amount of "fight" that the material puts up against the current flowing through it. During his telegraphy work, Edison had discovered something very interesting about the resistance of graphite – the type of pure carbon used for pencil leads. He had found that, if carbon was put under physical pressure, its resistance decreased. Naturally, varying amounts of pressure produced varying amounts of resistance. So the strength of any current flowing through the carbon would vary too.

This was it: a scientific breakthrough, and a practical alternative to the magnet-and-coil transmitting device used by Bell. If a diaphragm vibrated against a block of carbon, it would produce all the variation in current that was needed. It would, of course, now need a supply of electricity – but Edison had an idea about that too.

Stepping up the power

His telephone, he decided, would be battery-powered – but the power would be much stronger than a battery could normally provide. To step the power up, he would use an induction coil, an iron

The inventor of the phonograph, with the team that helped him produce, improve, and sell it. Charles Batchelor, Edison's colleague, is standing second from the left. Colonel Gouraud, who drummed up sensational publicity for Edison in Britain, is seated on the right. Edison relied heavily on his team-workers, especially on Batchelor and John Kreusi. Both men were outstandingly clever with their hands, so they could create the machines dreamed up by their clumsy-fingered boss.

bar wrapped in a *double* coil of wire. One of these two coiled wires led to and from the battery. The other, which had more turns in it, was joined to the telephone apparatus. When the current in the first coil was switched on and off, it induced a much more powerful current in the second one. With this double-coil device, Edison had found a simple way of making a current strong enough to carry the human voice over long distances.

Night birds

But he still had to get the transmitter right. At his new Menlo Park laboratory, he and his team worked tirelessly, hunting for the best way of using carbon to make a signal. Always a night bird, Edison would start work at nightfall, break for "lunch" at midnight, then go on till daybreak. Batchelor, his chief lieutenant, did the same.

Weary as his assistants became, they had an

32

easier job than their boss. They could *hear* what they were doing. They could tell at once if something was working . Edison could not. Sometimes he relied on what his team said. Sometimes he overcame his disability by using, not his ears, but ... his teeth. A magnet linked to the telephone circuit vibrated against them. The vibrations passed through the bones of Edison's jaw and straight to his undamaged inner ears. Doggedly, with clenched teeth and ringing head, the deaf inventor worked his way through hundreds upon hundreds of night-time experiments.

And then, in 1877, he suddenly found what he was looking for. One day in November, he chanced to look at a shard of glass from an old, broken oil lamp, lying out in the yard. Curiously, he turned it over. The glass was thick with lampblack: black, sticky soot, velvety smooth between his fingers. Was this, not graphite, the sort of carbon he needed? He told Batchelor, his most talented team-mate, to make some of the lampblack into a little flat cake, like a button.

Edison in later life, here seen with the instrument that he helped to perfect. Among the changes that he made to Bell's invention was the separation of earpiece and mouthpiece. Although telephone design has altered a great deal since this picture was taken, the separate earpiece and mouthpiece still survive.

"Splendid"

The moment came for the researchers to try the "button" out: just another experiment, like the two thousand or more they'd already done. The little cake was transferred onto a flat metal plate. Gently, another plate was put in position on top, and the diaphragm on top of that. Then the current was switched on ...

"Splendid," was how Edison later described the results of that night. The transmitter with the lamp-black button worked brilliantly, perfectly. The sound was much clearer than Bell's original tele-phone – the volume much louder. Even Edison himself could hear it.

Edison and the team had done it! For himself and his new invention factory, Edison had earned $100,000, paid by a delighted Western Union.

For the world, he had produced a telephone transmitter that, in its essentials, is the same as the one we use every time we make a phone call.

It was on November 9, 1877 that the inventor, now aged thirty, had the idea that brought him Western Union's huge reward. But the four weeks that followed were golden in more ways than one. During them, as work on the telephone transmitter reached its climax, *Edison also produced the phonograph.*

Off and on, he'd been working on it for months. This was nothing unusual, for he loved having several projects on the go at once. If he got stuck on one thing, he'd turn to another. If he got stuck there, too, he'd turn to a third. As often as not, an answer to his first problem would then pop into his head.

A toy for Marion

During the summer, just for fun, he'd made a toy for his five-year-old daughter, Marion. It was a model of a man sawing wood, with an odd-looking funnel on top. Round-eyed, Marion stared at it.

Electric light bulbs of Edison's own design still light the big laboratory on the upper floor of Menlo Park's main building: the birthplace of the telephone transmitter, the phonograph, and the electric light bulb itself. Night after night, Edison and his team would work here through the small hours, breaking for supper at midnight. The midnight feasts were cheerful affairs, with songs, imitations of the phonograph, and tunes played on the organ at the end of the room.

Opposite: Edison created the phonograph from a toy made for his daughter, Marion. This speaking doll has a miniature phonograph inside it so that the doll can "speak".

What did it do? Her father grinned at her, cleared his throat, and loudly recited a nonsense rhyme down the funnel. Busily, the little model started sawing wood. The model's machinery was linked to a diaphragm, like the ones Edison was using for the telephone transmitter. When someone shouted into the toy's funnel-shaped mouthpiece, the diaphragm's vibrations set the machinery in motion. No electric power was needed: the human voice was power enough.

The phonograph

The phonograph, when it emerged a few months later, took this idea several stages further. Edison noticed that, if he shouted at a diaphragm with a pin mounted on it, he could make marks on a piece of coated paper. He also noticed that, if the paper was pulled under the pin again, it made a sound:

"My plan was to synchronize the camera and the phonograph so as to record sounds when the pictures were made, and reproduce the two in harmony.... We did a lot of work along this line, and my talking pictures were shown in many theatres in the United States and foreign countries.... We had the first of the so-called 'Talking Pictures' in our laboratory thirty years ago."

Edison, recalling the birth of the Kinetoscope in 1925.

a sound that perhaps sounded like words.

In both the United States and France, other scientists had begun to work on the idea of turning the vibrations of the human voice into marks on a hard surface. By November, Edison knew he would have to act fast to protect the exploratory work he'd already done. By December 4, he had given Kreusi puzzling directions to build a machine with a grooved cylinder, flanked by its twin diaphragms and needles. By December 6, the machine was ready. "Mary's little lamb" was about to become the first vocal record ever made.

The needle in the furrow

This was how the phonograph worked. Edison's voice, as it recited the rhyme, made the recording diaphragm vibrate. Meanwhile, under the diaphragm's needle, the cylinder moved along with the needle itself following the tinfoil-covered groove cut in the brass. As the diaphragm moved out and in, the needle pressed harder or more gently on

Whatever will the man think of next? In this cartoon of 1878, the British magazine, "Punch", pokes sly fun at Edison's seemingly endless powers of invention. To this day, anti-gravity underwear still remains a dream rather than a reality. But an Edison of the future might enjoy meeting the challenge!

EDISON'S ANTI–GRAVITATION UNDER–CLOTHING

Tommy. „Oh! Don't wind us in yet, Mamma! It's so jolly up here, and not a bit cold!"

the tinfoil moving underneath it. In this way, all the sounds in "Mary's little lamb" were translated into alterations in the depth of the furrow carved in the tinfoil. To translate them back, they just needed to be transferred again to the diaphragm, via its attached needle. The diaphragm vibrated ... and Edison's high-pitched voice, captured from the past, sent shivers chasing up and down the backs of his loyal helpers.

"The Wizard of Menlo Park"

The machine that brought back the past caused an instant sensation. Its inventor, who had never lost the habit of thinking like a newsman, wasted no time in breaking the story. On December 7, 1877 he took the phonograph to the office of the journal, *Scientific American*, and played it to the editor and his staff. Instantly, the scene from the Menlo laboratory repeated itself. The audience was stunned, incredulous, then wild with enthusiasm.

Reading the news in their papers, the rest of the world joined in. The French called him "this astonishing Edison". The British, who had often pooh-poohed him as a mere technician, hailed him as a discoverer. In the United States President Hayes demanded to hear the new invention at the White House. And ordinary Americans, fascinated by both the machine and its thirty-year-old creator, turned him into a hero. From then on he was, in their words, "the Wizard of Menlo Park".

And now the light bulb

Blinking in the strong October sunlight, two men stepped out into the windy yard. With slow, measured steps, they walked the short space between Menlo Park's main laboratory and the glass-blower's shed, just behind it. One, carrying something in his hands, was Charles Batchelor. The other was the Wizard of Menlo himself. It was 1879 – less than two years after Edison had made his great breakthroughs in sound technology. Now he was aiming at something even bigger.

Still walking as if they were treading egg-shells, the two men entered the shed, paced across to a workbench – and stopped dead. Savagely, Edison cursed. Batchelor stared down at what he now held; two pieces of wire and two slender lengths of hard, dark material, curved like a horseshoe. A broken horseshoe.

The pair turned round and trudged back to the lab. On one of its tables, among the scientific clutter, lay a reel of sewing thread. Edison seized it and cut off a small piece. Carefully, he fastened each end of the tiny thread to a piece of platinum wire, then coaxed it to lie in a groove cut inside a metal block. Covering it with another piece of metal, he slid the metal block into a furnace.

Making the electric light bulb

There was a long wait. Batchelor slumped in a chair. Edison vanished to one of the dark corners where he caught up on missing sleep. Both men were exhausted. They had been up all the night before, and the one before that. As for going home: Edison hadn't been near the place for days.

Opposite: The light that lasted: an Edison light bulb demonstrates its tawny glow for a modern photographer. Edison would later recall that, before achieving his great breakthrough with electric lighting, he constructed no less than three thousand separate theories to cover its workings. By tireless experimenting, he whittled the three thousand down to two. After establishing that a carbon filament worked, he then carbonized six thousand different types of material to decide which one worked best.

The same principle, different materials. The tungsten filament in this modern light bulb heats up when an electric current passes through it. This makes the wire glow. In his experiments over a hundred years ago, Edison thought of using tungsten himself. But the technology did not then exist to let him carry this experiment out.

> "The first step is an intuition – and comes with a burst, **then** difficulties arise. – This thing gives out and then that – 'Bugs' – as such little faults and difficulties are called – show themselves and months of anxious watching, study and labor are requisite before commercial success or failure – is certainly reached.... I have the right principle and am on the right tracks, but time, hard work, and some good luck are necessary too."
>
> Thomas Edison, describing his inventive process, in 1878.

At last, late in the afternoon, the cotton in its metal case was ready. Sweating with tension, the two men opened the case and gently extracted the delicate carbon horseshoe that the thread had now become. The next stage was to enclose it in a glass globe. All the air would then be pumped out of the globe so that the horseshoe was surrounded by a vacuum. The Menlo Park team was trying to make an electric lamp – or, as we'd call it today, an electric light bulb.

If Edison's plans worked out, a current flowing through the carbonized cotton would make it glow with a clear, steady light. And, in that vacuum, the light would last. In the light bulbs that other inventors were trying to make, the glowing filament burned out within a few minutes. But a carbonized cotton filament was different. Or it would be different – if only they could make one. Surely, they'd succeeded this time.

But they hadn't. Lightning-fast, disaster struck. One careless movement, and a screwdriver came tumbling from its place on the crowded bench. As the two men watched in horror, it fell against the fragile carbon horseshoe. And, once again, the carbon broke.

Numbly, the experimenters repeated the procedure: cotton, wires, metal case, furnace. And then the long, long wait, with heads aching and minds blank with fatigue. At last, the third carbon of the day was ready. Yawning and gritty-eyed, Edison and his companion freed it from its case, carried it across the yard and, finally, enclosed it in the safety of a waiting glass globe. The pump was set to work. Little by little, all but the minutest amount of air was driven out of the globe. By 1:30 a.m. the next morning, the globe was ready and waiting.

The light that lasted

As the laboratory workers watched, the electric current was turned on. And there, like a tawny starburst, was the light! Everyone held their breath – and then, as the light stayed on, slowly breathed out again. The light was still on an hour later. Two hours. Three...

Dawn came, bringing the promise of another hot, dry October day. The glow of the carbon filament paled in the growing light, but still it burned. Full of hope, and with all fatigue forgotten, Edison and the rest watched it joyously. By 3 p.m., when the lamp's glass cracked, the filament had burned for over thirteen hours.

That Christmas, the "Wizard" lit up his home and laboratory with dozens of his new lights. In the midwinter darkness, Menlo Park glowed like a vision, with lamps lining the road and gleaming from the windows. Thousands of visitors from all over the United States poured in to Menlo Park, jostling each other, ooh-ing and aah-ing.

This was only the start, Edison told them. He planned to light up New York itself.

A rival to gaslight

Edison's interest in electric light went back further than his triumphs with sound. But he only started to pay it full attention in 1878 when, after all the frenzied work of the year before, he felt tired, let down and in need of a change. Right from the start, he had a clear idea of what he planned to achieve. He intended to create a rival to the United States' multi-million dollar gas industry. Because they had no competition, the gas companies often did just as they pleased – with no regard for the law nor people's rights. Their domination was causing a growing feeling of resentment among the general public. If possible, Edison was going to put that industry out of business.

In the U.S.A., gas made from coal had been used for streets and public buildings since very early in the nineteenth century. It was distributed by pipes laid under the streets. By Edison's time, city-dwellers lit their homes with it too, while some up-to-date households also used it for cooking. Rural areas everywhere depended on much more primitive lighting systems, such as oil lamps, which were expensive and smelled, and candles. Neither could light a house really well.

Today, oil lamps like these are regarded as antiques: interesting, decorative, and useful in a power-cut! For the people of Edison's time, they were a vital part of everyday life. They were also smoky, smelly, hard to read by and – if knocked over – an appalling fire risk. When the oil-lamps were brought out, the day was more or less over. But, with Edison's electric lighting system, it could be extended far into the night.

A romantic glow – or the dinginess of a winter afternoon? This memory of gaslit London in the nineteenth century has the same nostalgic charm as the Victorian oil-lamp.

In deciding to beat the gas industry at its own game, Edison had set himself a task that seemed superhuman. His goal was nothing less than the creation of a complete power system. The way he was planning it, homes using electric light would be linked to a central power station, just as they already were to gas plants. And the link would not be made with pipes, but with shining copper wire: miles upon miles of copper wire, holding a whole city in its web.

The first priority

At that time the only electric lamps in use were arc lights: big lamps in which an electric current was made to jump across a gap between two pieces of carbon. The arc light was invented in Britain by Sir Humphry Davy in 1812, some time before Edison decided to improve things. It was *the* alternative to gas. But it was restricted in its use to streetlighting mainly because of the glare of the light and also the smell and smoke that it produced. The lights were wired in a series, or group, in a pattern which resembles the beads on a necklace. As the current flowed through the wire it passed through every arc light; it was not possible, therefore, to turn one single light off by itself. The whole series had to be turned off and on together.

Edison's first priority was clear. He had to get electricity to all the lamps owned by large numbers of individual subscribers. And each subscriber had to be able to turn any single lamp off and on at any moment. This meant that the lamps had to be wired up in a special way: a way that few people had so far tried. Electrical wiring has to take the form of a closed loop, or circuit, leading both from a power source and back to it. The wiring pattern Edison decided to use was called a parallel circuit. The wiring diagram for this looked, not like a necklace, but a ladder. On each of the ladder's rungs was a light. The current flowed down one of the ladder's uprights and back up the other. It also flowed across the rungs, feeding the lights – *as long as the lights were turned on*. If a light was turned off, the current "missed" that rung, and continued on its way round and across the rest of the circuit.

Ohm's law

But this was where money got in the way. The first plans Edison drew up involving parallel circuits used far, far too much copper wire. Setting up such a system would have bankrupted anyone who tried it. Somehow, those costs had to be dragged down.

Edison boasted of not understanding one of the basic laws of electricity, named after the German scientist, Georg Ohm. But, in spite of that, he triumphantly used Ohm's Law to solve the huge problem that faced him. Ohm's Law helps people to work out the mathematics involved in setting up an electrical circuit. It says there is a connection between the size (or strength) of a current, the amount of resistance in the substance it flows through, and the force that makes the current flow. This force

Gas was first used for lighting in the late eighteenth century, and this quick-footed lamplighter still wears eighteenth-century costume. He needed the ladder to climb up to each lamp. After lighting it, he'd climb down and race on to the next one. People still talk of "running like a lamplighter" – and square-sided gaslamps like these were still being used in Britain as late as the 1950s. By then, lamplighters did their rounds on bicycles!

"We are striking it big in the electric light, better than my vivid imagination first conceived. Where this thing is going to stop Lord only knows!"

Thomas Edison, writing in October 1879.

– the "push" behind the current – is measured in units called volts. The units describing a current's strength are called amperes. Resistance is measured in units called ohms, after Ohm himself. Ohm's law says that the size of the current depends on the amount of force behind it, divided by the amount of resistance involved.

Cutting the costs

Edison worked out that, to cut his copper costs, he had to cut the size of the current he used. But parallel circuits usually needed a strong current. Could he make a smaller, weaker current do the same job? Ohm's law provided the answer. The inventor could "economize" on current – and on wire – if he built more resistance into the circuit. Until then, everyone had been working to produce lamps that worked with low-resistance filaments. Edison decided to do the exact opposite. He started with carbon, which has a very high resistance, but it burned out before the right temperature was reached. He then moved on to platinum, but it melted when it was heated to the right temperature needed to give a bright light. When he discovered how to get a very high vacuum in his light bulbs, using a Sprengel pump to force the air out, he went back to experimenting with carbon again.

The very high vacuum meant that more air – and therefore more oxygen – had been removed from inside the bulb, which prevented the filament from burning out so quickly. It had been the low vacuum – leaving more oxygen inside the bulb – that had caused the carbon filament to burn out too soon.

With his triumph in October 1879, Edison knew he was over one of the worst hurdles. Thanks to his cotton carbon filament, he knew he could distribute electric power at a businesslike price.

"Long-waisted Mary Ann"

By this time, he'd also solved another of the problems facing him: how to *produce* the electricity his new system would need. He'd use a generator, or

Holborn Viaduct, one of the first London streets to be lit by electricity.

dynamo – a machine that, using Faraday's discovery about converting movement into electricity, turned steam power into electric power. To make his calculations work, the dynamo had to produce current of a constant voltage and it had to be economical. At the time, all dynamos were extremely inefficient. They wasted almost two-thirds of the energy used to make them work. Naturally, Edison wanted to do better than that! So he set about designing his own, more efficient dynamo.

In the summer of 1879, he and his team succeeded. The dynamo they built looked like nothing engineers had ever seen before. Edison's men, remembering a pretty visitor to the lab, coined a nickname for the towering monster they'd made. She became the "Long-waisted Mary Ann".

"He could go to sleep anywhere, any time, on anything. I have seen him asleep on a work bench with his arm for a pillow; in a chair with his feet on his desk; on a cot with all his clothes on. I have seen him sleep for thirty-six hours at a stretch, interrupted for only an hour while he consumed a large steak, potatoes and pie, and smoked a cigar, and I have known him go to sleep standing on his feet."

Thomas Edison remembered by his colleague Alfred O. Tate.

All aboard!

Linked to a steam engine in a room behind, the "Mary Ann" proved herself brilliantly efficient. She converted steam into electricity with a loss of no more than a fifth of the energy involved. Always

Worn out by a long night of work, Edison takes a catnap on a laboratory bench.

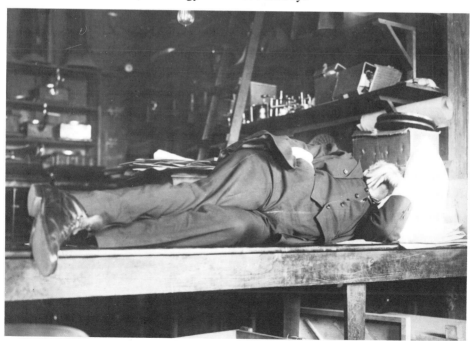

45

enchanted by a change of project, Edison soon worked out an extra way to use his wonderful new machine. In 1880, he used it to drive the United States' first full-size electric train.

The year before, the German company, Siemans, had demonstrated one at the Berlin Trade Fair. The "Wizard of Menlo" decided to test his own. He had metal rails laid around the Menlo Park grounds and – shelving his great lighting project for a minute – converted a "Mary Ann" dynamo into an electric motor.

On May 13, all was ready. Edison ordered the power to be switched on and, with boyish delight, he climbed aboard the train. Visitors and staff followed, packing themselves into the little carriage wherever they could. Batchelor, on the beer crate that was the driver's seat, switched the engine on, and off they went: bouncing, jouncing and clinging on for dear life as the train rattled round curves and over bumps at twenty-five miles an hour. The return journey was less exciting. The engine broke down, and the passengers had to get out and push.

The railway was another success for Edison and in September 1881, the Electric Railway Company of America was founded. But Edison soon had to vanish back into the complex world of electric light, and the company failed to prosper.

Opposite top: Edison's second laboratory at West Orange, New Jersey. At Menlo Park and here, the inventor and his team ran the world's first-ever industrial research operation. Edison thought of his two labs as "invention factories". The West Orange one was much bigger than its predecessor. All the better, said its owner; it meant that inventions could be perfected in days, rather than months.

Will the lamps come on?

It was quarter to three in the afternoon of September 4, 1882. Down on Pearl Street, in grimy lower Manhattan, the men sweated in New York's summer heat. Throughout the building at Number 255, tension screamed in the air. In the nearby financial district, it also filled the Wall Street offices of the great banker, J.P. Morgan.

Nervously, the directors of the Edison Electric Light Company kept taking out their watches, looking at them, pocketing them again. Then, looking around the room, they solemnly eyed the waiting lights, with their shining glass globes. The lights were connected by underground wires to the Pearl Street building, which now housed the very heart

Opposite bottom: The chemistry lab in the "inventions factory", where rows of chemicals still bear witness to the huge amount of testing that went on. The search for the telephone transmitter alone took over two thousand experiments; the development of the electric light bulb involved many thousands more.

47

Proof of Edison's success. By 1890 this Edison power station, with its giant dynamos, workshops and offices, was supplying subscribers in Brooklyn, across the East River from its famous parent on Pearl Street. Only eight years before, when the Pearl Street station itself was opened, it had – in Edison's own words – "no parallel in the world".

of Edison's electric lighting scheme: the power station that would supply electricity to all the scheme's subscribers. At 3:00 p.m., the great generator at Pearl Street would be set in action. In offices and other buildings around the area, four hundred "Edison lamps" would come on.

Or would they?

Edison waits

Dazzlingly smart in a brand-new coat, Edison paced the Wall Street office floor. Ceaselessly, the events of the past four years whirled round and round in his brain: the false starts, the struggles, the triumphs. And the moments of sheer horror – like the time in July when, suddenly, the Pearl Street generators had run amok.

Then there were all the fights. There had been fights about money; fights with the threatened gas companies; fights with other scientists, disbelieving what he'd done, or claiming they'd got there first. Well, Edison thought as he paced, nothing new in that. It was always happening – someone popping up and grabbing at all the credit. Anyway, to the devil with the lot of them.

Abruptly, the inventor's thoughts darted off in another direction: back to the generators. For safety, they were only using one. But would it work? Suppose it went mad again, screeching like a thousand banshees? Would the men know what to do? They had no experience in running a central power station. And yet ... and yet....

Thomas Alva Edison – usually so bold, so confident, so full of spark and bounce and go – was, for once, afraid.

On all the clocks and watches, the hour hand slowly dragged round to three. Again, all eyes turned to the Edison lamps. Time, for a second, seemed to stand still.

And then, inside the glass globes, a tiny curl of light appeared: a curl like a horseshoe. Swiftly, the glowing light gathered strength, then shone out brightly. The work of dozens and dozens of dedicated scientists who'd worked on electricity over decades had been worthwhile. Edison's great gamble had succeeded. It was three o'clock, and the Age of Electricity had begun.

By evening, Edison's signature gleamed across lower New York: electric lights in counting rooms, and newspaper offices, and private houses, all giving out their soft, radiant light. Their creator, meanwhile, was no longer the spruce but anguished figure that had paced the floor of Morgan's office. With collar gone and his white felt hat smudged with dirt, Edison had reverted to his rumpled, bustling self. He'd spent part of the afternoon down a street manhole, hunting for a fuse that had blown.

The rich businessman

After the lights came on that September afternoon, Edison summed up his feelings in a very few words. "I have," he told reporters, "accomplished all that I promised." Unlike many of his remarks to the

"The Pearl Street station was the biggest and most responsible thing I had ever undertaken. It was a gigantic problem, with many ramifications.... Success meant world-wide adoption of our central-station plan. Failure meant loss of money and prestige and setting back of our enterprise. All I can remember of the events of that day is that I had been up most of the night rehearsing my men and going over every part of the system.... If I ever did any thinking in my life it was on that day."
Thomas Edison, recalling
September 4, 1882.

The lights of New York, here shown aiding millions of office workers to do their jobs. But the benefits of electricity go much further than this. Without an efficient supply of power to light their homes, warm them and help keep them clean, these people would actually be leading shorter lives, and so would millions of others. The improvement in home living conditions over the past century has been a major contribution to the doubling of life expectancy in the West.

press, this was no boast but the plain, unvarnished truth. The Pearl Street light-up marked the pinnacle of his achievements.

Oddly enough, it did not bring him the huge fame that the phonograph had. The Edison of Pearl Street, who had given the world a new energy system to use, was an engineer and businessman. He did not have the charisma of the Wizard of Menlo. Besides, the new lighting system took time to catch on. But, at the end of the 1880s, fame came back with a rush – and the cause, as before, was the phonograph.

By this time, Edison's life had changed a great deal. For a start, he was rich; very rich. He had left his Menlo Park base and was now building a new one, at West Orange. And he had a new wife.

Mary – lonely, sweet-natured Mary – died in 1884 from typhoid. Two years later, Edison, now aged thirty-nine, married a beautiful, sophisticated girl named Mina Miller. Mina, who came from a wealthy family, hoped to "house-train" her tobacco-chewing, work-obsessed husband. Throughout their lives together, she would always be trying to make him behave in a way that fitted his wealth and status. Much as Edison loved her, she seldom succeeded!

Improving the phonograph

In 1887, for the second time in his life, Edison found himself jolted into a new project by the work of the inventor of the telephone, Alexander Graham Bell. Bell had produced a phonograph of his own, but he recognized the contribution Edison had made with his own phonograph. So – much more willing to share his work than Edison – he suggested to Edison that they should join forces and market the new machine under their joint names.

Edison was enraged. He decided to resurrect the forgotten machine he had built ten years before, rather than allow anyone to share the credit of the invention. He worked on it for a year. Once he'd started, the businessman found he was delighted to be back at the workbench. Jettisoning the fragile tinfoil of earlier days, he used all wax cylinders for his recording surface. With a sapphire for a needle, and a more sophisticated pick-up head, the machine worked better. Edison, by now very deaf, struggled to make it work better still. He went back to his old method of sound-testing. If all else failed, he'd bite desperately on the machine's amplifying equipment, hoping to feel the sounds that could not penetrate his ears.

Edison's second wife, Mina. Only recently-widowed, the inventor fell in love with her at first sight when he met her in 1885. Unlike his first wife, Mary, Mina did sometimes manage to make Edison listen to her. Once, he refused to eat the dinner she sent over to the West Orange lab. She marched straight in, and stood over him until he finished it.

The entertainment machine

Edison had always seen the phonograph as an aid to business. He thought it could be used for dictating letters and before long many businesses in the United States were using it for just this purpose.

"He invents all the while, even in his dreams."
Mina Edison, describing her husband.

But, once the machine had been put on the market, the public thought differently. High-brow listeners were charmed by the magic machine that, in the comfort of the drawing-room, reproduced the sound of a choir, an orchestra and an organ, playing Handel for all they were worth. Children loved the Edison talking dolls, which recited nursery rhymes ("Mary's lamb" included). And the general public flocked to push coins into an early version of the juke-box, the nickelodeon.

Whatever its inventor may have planned, the true role of the "sound-writer" was to entertain. It still is. The phonograph was replaced by Emile Berliner's disc record and gramophone. But nothing can destroy Edison's place as the man who, in the 1870s and '80s, gave sound recording to the world.

With scarcely a pause, Edison then went on to add moving pictures to the sound.

Portrait of the inventor as a hero. In this carefully-posed photograph, taken in 1888 and later used as an advertisement, Edison slumps beside his improved version of the phonograph. The public was told that he had worked on it for five days without sleep. (The total was in fact three.) Edison was a gifted public relations officer for his own inventions. It helped that he was also photogenic!

Moving pictures

By the 1880s, there had already been many attempts to produce pictures that moved. Since the 1830s, people had known that an impression of movement could be produced if the eye moved quickly over a series of pictures. Each picture showed one tiny stage of motion: a horse trotting, for instance, or a woman jumping off a chair. If all the pictures were viewed in ultra-fast sequence, the viewer would see a blurry horse … trotting.

The earliest of these "moving" pictures were drawings. By Edison's time, a British photographer, Eadweard Muybridge, was doing the same thing with photographs. Each one was taken by a different – still – camera, using glass photographic plates. One minute of the trotting horse film needed over seven hundred cameras to shoot! Muybridge met Edison in 1888, and they discussed making phonograph records to go with the photographs. The idea was dropped because Muybridge didn't think the phonograph was loud enough to use with a large audience.

But Muybridge's visit had given Edison an idea.

The inventor, who was working on his phonograph at the same time, naturally had cylinders on his mind. He decided to coat one in light-sensitive material and to use it inside a camera. With every picture taken, the cylinder turned on slightly. When the "film" was developed, the cylinder had a spiral of little photographs running round it. If it was then twirled round in a viewer, the resulting picture seemed to move. Coining a name for his new invention, he called it the "kinetoscope".

Edison was not the only person working on the moving picture idea. In Britain, another photographer, William Friese-Greene, was experimenting with the new celluloid film produced by the American inventor George Eastman. A Frenchman was using a stop-and-start film made of paper.

In 1889, Edison got hold of some Eastman film himself, made up – as he'd asked – into long strips. Very soon, he had built a camera that would feed the long filmstrip through at a steady rate. To view the developed film, he invented a new peepshow-type viewer to go with it. At the same time he was thinking about projecting the films he shot onto large screens, but he rejected the idea. He had a movie studio built at West Orange, where he shot films of boxers, dancers and circus turns. But when he had his invention patented, he did not extend the patent to outside the U.S.A. He also forgot to mention the idea of projection.

In 1894, a Frenchman called Lumière bought an Edison kinetoscope and gave it to his sons. The Lumières, who were photographers, adapted the Edison kinetoscope to take a projector and, in 1895, opened the first public cinema. And so it was the Lumières who were the first people to bring cinema to large-scale audiences – with an Edison kinetoscope as the base of their system.

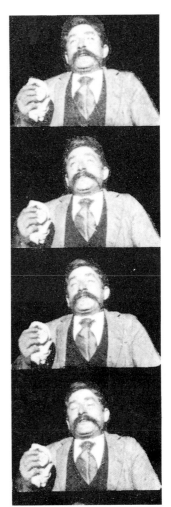

Frames from "The Sneeze", one of the first movies ever made. The star of this kinetoscope "short" was John Ott, a member of Edison's team since the Newark days. The movie had its own sound-effects (recorded on the phonograph), so the world's earliest films were far from silent.

The luck begins to fade

Edison was forty-four when, in 1891, he applied for his patent on the kinetoscope. He was almost exactly half-way through his life. During the next forty years, his reputation grew and grew. Already one of the most famous Americans alive, he turned into a living legend in the twentieth century.

"It [electricity] is so easy of control, the apparatus required so inexpensive, that it can be used as a motor power for purposes innumerable. In a house it can be used to drive miniature fans for cooling purposes, to operate a sewing machine, to pump water, to work a dumb waiter or an elevator, and for a hundred other domestic uses which now require personal labor."
Thomas Edison, writing in the "Boston Herald", in 1885.

"I constructed a helicopter but I couldn't get it light enough."
Edison, recalling the 1880s.

He was the Grand Old Man of science, the friend of presidents and of great industrialists like Henry Ford. But he was still plain, wise-cracking Al Edison: the man who chewed tobacco, spat, told funny stories and, with his forgetfulness and his homespun ways, drove his patient wife to despair. Like a Wild West character from the movies he'd help create, he was an all-American hero.

A hero, yes; but what had happened to the inventor? Sadly, his heyday was already over. Very slowly and gently, Edison's luck – the "magic touch" for which the Wizard of Menlo was renowned – began to dry up. True, his actual inventiveness never faltered. Tirelessly, the ideas still poured out, and their owner still investigated them with glee. But the triumphs and happy endings became rarer.

Losing a fortune

Was Edison disappointed? He was. But, always shy of showing his inmost feelings, he would laugh his disappointment off. During the 1890s, for instance, he lost a fortune on a project to extract iron from the low-grade ore deposits on the east coast of the United States. He built his own mine in New Jersey, and invented the machinery to work it. Then, by the worst of luck, high-grade ore deposits were discovered elsewhere that could be mined more cheaply. The price of iron plummeted; Edison's project went bust, taking two million dollars with it. "Well," said its owner soon after, "it's all gone, but we had a hell of a good time spending it."

Never one to say die, he later used his mining expertise to set up a cement works. In a short while, he had revolutionized the way cement was made and experimented with making concrete roads, then concrete houses. The road-making project, though a failure, was linked to something else that came much closer to success: the production of an electric car.

Edison would not have been Edison if he had not got involved in the development of the automobile. It was also the automobile that forged his friendship with Henry Ford. The two first met in

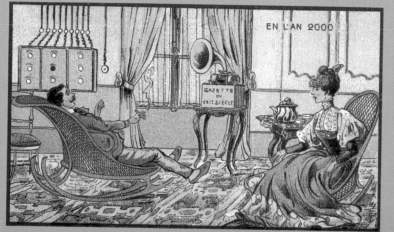

"Visions of the Year 2000", drawn at the very end of the nineteenth century: a dictating machine, an electrical floor-cleaner, and the audio-newspaper that relates the latest news to its well-dressed listeners. Thanks to Edison, all three dreams have come true – even if their appearance differs from the versions shown here! The dictaphone and the electric cleaner emerged directly from Edison's work. He did not invent the equipment that made today's radio broadcasts possible. But his experiments paved the way for the man who did: Ambrose Fleming, inventor of the radio valve or electron tube.

Fast friends, Henry Ford and Al Edison take a ride in one of Ford's own cars. This photograph was taken when Edison's inventive luck had all but run out. However, he was able to bask in the fame his earlier achievements had brought him, and enjoy the friendship of the United States' leading figures.

1896, the year Ford brought out his first car. Ford deeply admired the older man, and the two got on brilliantly. Edison applauded Ford's description of his petrol-fuelled vehicle. But then, on his own account, Edison began to work on plans for a battery-driven car instead.

For ten years, he worked at producing a storage battery that would keep a car going for a hundred miles, with a cruising speed of twenty-five mph. It cost him a million dollars. At last, in 1909, he was satisfied. The battery was ready to be sold, and some firms brought out electric cars and trucks that used it. But, just as had happened with the iron-works, the great inventor was wretchedly unlucky with his timing.

No giving up

The year before, Ford had produced the famous "tin lizzie": the cheap, petrol-fuelled Model-T, which brought the car within the reach of ordinary pockets and families. From then on, the link between the car and the petrol engine was unbreakable. Edison had come on the scene just too late.

Again, he did not give up. By 1912, at Ford's request, he was applying his hard-earned knowledge to designing a battery-powered self-starter for the Model-T itself. He was still vainly struggling with this task and still working sixteen hours a day in the 1920s, when he was over seventy. But, by that time, a happy ending to the whole saga of the storage batteries had unexpectedly appeared. Used for other purposes, they were making a lot of money. They had fulfilled Edison's prime aim, worked out so many years before: to invent things that would *sell.*

A fitting tribute?

On a fine October night in 1931, Edison died , aged eighty-four: killed by diabetes, kidney disease, a gastric ulcer and a lifetime of punishingly hard work. Plans were quickly made to pay the dead hero some special tribute. He had brought the use of electricity to the nation's homes. On the day of his funeral, it was proposed that the nation should mourn him by turning its electricity off.

Instantly, it was realized that it couldn't be done.

The United States without electricity: it was impossible. In factories, machinery would have come shuddering to a halt. Electric trains would have stopped running. Oil wells would have stopped pumping. In the buildings that towered above the city streets, people would be marooned halfway to the sky: the lifts that made skyscrapers possible would have all stopped too. And what about all the hospitals that relied on electricity for their light and equipment? And the offices? The growing numbers of farms? And all the millions of homes?

The plans were hurriedly changed. President Hoover proposed that mourners should, if they wanted, turn off any lights that were not essential. With all their hearts, Americans everywhere agreed. So, on the evening of October 21, 1931, a great shadow swept across the country, like an eclipse. Even the Statue of Liberty briefly held a darkened torch aloft.

"An inventor frequently wastes his time and his money trying to extend his invention to uses for which it is not at all suitable. Edison has never done this. He rides no hobbies. He views each problem that comes up as a thing of itself, to be solved in exactly the right way.... His knowledge is so nearly universal that he cannot be classed as an electrician or a chemist – in fact, Mr. Edison cannot be classified.... The more I have seen of him the greater he has appeared to me – both as a servant of humanity and as a man."
Henry Ford.

Above: Producing the sound of the past: the phonograph needle as we know it today. Shown here many times magnified, the diamond stylus of a modern record-player rests lightly in the spiral groove of a record, responding to variations carved by sound in the groove's sides. Again, the modern versions are directly descended from Edison's discoveries.

Opposite: State of the art: electronic equipment in a present-day laboratory in Germany. The process that led to its manufacture and use started in 1880, when Edison was developing the electric light bulb.

Edison: the legacy

The debate over his memorial shows something of what Thomas Alva Edison left behind him. But only something. Some inventors who have changed the world did so with just one invention: their life's work. Edison, in contrast, could number his creations in dozens, even in hundreds. An extraordinary mixture of visionary and practical man, he invented because he could not help himself. To him, invention was as natural as breathing, and the list of what he achieved is staggering in its length and complexity. In all, he took out 1093 patents on his work.

For each of his famous achievements – the phonograph and electric light – there are several less well-known ones that, in their essentials, looked ahead to the way we live today. The phonograph doubled as the first dictaphone. Linked with the telephone as the "telescribe", it was also the first answering machine. His prefabricated concrete houses found an echo in later building methods.

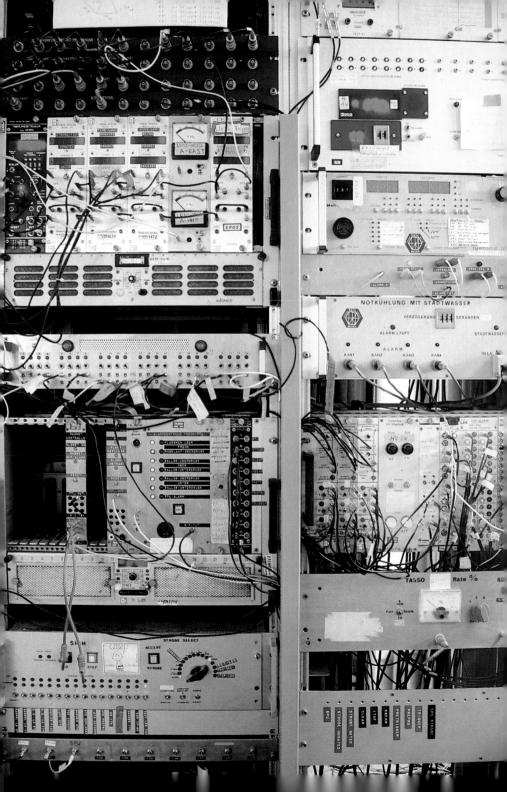

Most important of all, there was his "Edison-effect" lamp, from which the foundations of the science of electronics grew.

Intrigued though he was by the mysteries of the "effect", the overworked inventor did not follow its implications up. It was the British engineer, Ambrose Fleming, who, in the early 1900s, used Edison's discovery to create the electronic radio valve. In the same way, many of Edison's own creations were built upon work that had been done earlier – sometimes only a few years earlier, even months – by other people.

Thanks, Mr. Edison

Throughout his life, Edison's rivals continually accused him of stealing their glory. He was quick to accuse them of the same thing. At that time, many people were working on similar projects, so it was, and is, extremely hard to find out who really did what first. All the same, we can certainly ask if the world would have been much different today if Edison – Edison himself, not his predecessors or rivals – had never lived.

It would not be right to say that, without him, we would still be living with gas-lamps, open fires and steam-powered sewing machines. Sooner or later, someone would probably have also designed a power system as effective as Edison's. Someone, too, would probably have turned Bell's telephone into a machine for practical use. It's less likely that someone would have invented the phonograph, which owed almost nothing to any other earlier work. Without the deaf Wizard of Menlo, we might still be in the age of the piano and the musical-box.

But "probably" isn't "definitely". We can never know for sure what our lives would have been like if Edison, the "Wizard", had never existed. We do, however, know they would have been different – perhaps very different. Edison's nickname was an apt one. Like an alchemist in a fable, his power lay in practical transformations: tinfoil into sound, cotton thread into light. Using what materials came to hand, he transformed the past into our present.

"I am convinced that wars not only will not cease but will be frequent until the controlling groups in all the countries conclude that war is far too hazardous an enterprise to be undertaken in any circumstance whatever."
Thomas Edison, in 1927.

"One day, we may harness the rise and fall of the tides and imprison the rays of the sun."
Thomas Edison, in 1922.

Important Dates

1847   February 11: Thomas Alva Edison is born in Milan, Ohio, USA.

1854   The Edison family move to Port Huron, Michigan. Soon after this, Edison catches scarlet fever, and is seriously ill. This illness may have been the initial cause of his later deafness.

1855   Edison spends three months in the school of the Rev. G.B. Engle.

1859   Edison, aged twelve, becomes a newsboy on the Detroit-Port Huron railway line.

1861   The American Civil War breaks out between the anti-slavery northern states, and the southern ones with their slave-based economy.

1862   The Battle of Shiloh; Edison uses the telegraph to market newspapers carrying news of the battle.

1863   Edison becomes a telegrapher at sixteen, and spends the next few years wandering from one telegraph job to another.

1868   Edison arrives in Boston, and takes a job at the Western Union Telegraph Company. He applies for his first patent (on the vote-recorder), and news of his duplex apparatus is written up in the telegraphers' trade journal.

1869   January: Edison sets up on his own as a free-lance inventor. He applies for his second patent, on improvements to the stock ticker.
April: Trials of his duplex apparatus fail.
October: Edison and Franklin L. Pope set up in partnership as electrical engineers.

1871   Edison establishes his manufacturing shop in Newark, New Jersey.
December: Thomas Edison marries Mary Stilwell.

1874   Edison successfully produces a new multi-message telegraph system, the quadruplex, which can send two messages from each end of the wire at the same time.

1876   January: Edison starts to set up a new laboratory, in the New Jersey village of Menlo Park, and moves in later in the year.
March: Alexander Graham Bell is granted a patent for his newly-invented telephone.

1877   January: Edison begins work on his carbon telephone transmitter.
November: Edison uses a lampblack "button" to make huge improvements in his carbon transmitter's effectiveness.
December: Edison creates the phonograph.

1878   Edison starts work on the electric light and a system for distributing electricity.

1879   Summer: The "Long-waisted Mary Ann" dynamo is designed.

1879   October: Edison discovers that a filament of carbonized cotton thread, placed in a high vacuum inside a glass glove, will give out many hours of light before burning out.

1880   An electric railway is built and used at Menlo Park.

1881   Edison leaves Menlo Park and moves back to New York.

1882	While working on the electric light, Edison notices a black deposit on the inside of the light bulb: first evidence of the "Edison effect". September 4: The power is switched on at the Pearl Street generating station, New York.
1884	Edison's wife, Mary, dies.
1886	Thomas Edison marries Mina Miller, and settles with her at "Glenmont", a big estate in the Orange Valley, New Jersey.
1887	Edison starts work on improving the phonograph; he also builds a large new laboratory at West Orange.
1888	Edison revives an iron-ore processing company started in the 1870s. Over the following years, he buys land in New Jersey with iron deposits, and sets up an ore-processing plant and a mining village.
1891	Edison patents his kinetoscope in the USA.
1899	Edison begins work on developing a battery for electric cars.
1900	Edison's work on iron-ore processing is finally dropped.
1902	Edison sets up a successful cement-works. (His road-making and house-building projects develop from this business.)
1912	Edison starts work on designing an electric self-starter for Henry Ford's Model-T, which has ousted electric cars from the market.
1914-1918	World War I. Edison spends much time working on scientific developments for the United Sates Navy.
1927	Edison sets up a laboratory in Florida to research home-grown sources of rubber, as an alternative to the usual Malayan product.
1931	August: Edison collapses, and is diagnosed as dangerously ill. October 18: Thomas Alva Edison dies, aged eighty-four. October 21: The USA turns off its lights in mourning.

Further reading

Clark, Ronald W.: *Edison: the man who made the future* (Macdonald and Jane's, London, 1977)

Conot, Robert: *A streak of luck: the life and legend of Thomas Alva Edison* (Seaview Books, New York, 1979) [It is important to read at least one adult biography of Thomas A. Edison. These are all excellent, but use their indexes to browse around the subject.]

Abbott, David (ed.): *The biographical dictionary of scientists: engineers and inventors* (Blond Educational, London, 1985)

Blotz, C.L.: *How it is made: electricity* (Faber and Faber, London, 1985)

Egan, Louise: *Thomas Edison: the great American inventor* (Barron's Educational Series, Hauppage, New York, 1987)

Heren, Louis: *The story of America* (Times Books, London, 1976) [A highly readable introduction to American history and social conditions.]

Scientific Terms

Ampere: The unit used for measuring the rate of flow of an electric current or its size (strength). It is named after André Ampère, who researched electromagnetism in the 1820s.

Battery: A source of electricity which works, not by converting movement into electricity, but by chemical reaction. The first battery, made by the Italian scientist Alessandro Volta, was made up of silver, zinc and wet cardboard which reacted on each other to produce an electric current.

Circuit: The closed-loop pattern used for electrical wiring. Circuits lead both from and back to the power source, passing through one or more electric appliances on the way.

Diaphragm: A thin, springy piece of material, often metal, which vibrates easily.

Duplex: A telegraphic system for sending two messages over the same wire. In the 1870s, Edison successfully developed a refinement, the "quadruplex", that sent four messages over the same wire – two from each end.

Dynamo: A machine that converts movement into electricity, using magnetic *induction* – is often called a generator. One well-known type of dynamo is the appliance that converts the movement of a cyclist's feet into electricity to light a bicycle lamp.

Edison effect: Edison's discovery of an electric current flowing from one leg of a light filament across the vacuum inside a light bulb, without wires to carry it. This finding, which pointed the way to the science of electronics, would later be of crucial importance to other scientists.

Electromagnet: A "temporary" magnet made out of a piece (or "core") of iron, wrapped in a coil of wire linked to an electric power source. When the current is turned on, the iron becomes a magnet. The first electromagnet was made by an Englishman named William Sturgeon in 1824.

Filament: The thread-like fitting inside a light bulb which, when the current is turned on, heats up and glows. Edison's first successful filament was made out of carbonized sewing thread; later, he used carbonized bamboo. Modern filaments are made of metal.

Induction, electromagnetic: The generation of electrical energy through movement, by changing the relative positions of a magnet and a coil of wire. This way of generating electricity was discovered by the scientist Michael Faraday in 1831.

Kinetoscope: The peepshow-type apparatus invented by Edison for viewing films made with his "kinetographic" (moving-picture) camera. "Kineto" comes from a Greek word for movement.

Membrane: A thin, stretchy piece of tissue, often skin.

Morse code: The communication system invented by American artist Samuel Morse in the 1830s, for use with the *telegraph* system he was developing. It consists of a mixture of short and long signals ("dots" and "dashes"). Each letter of the alphabet is assigned its own code value.

Ohm: The unit used for measuring electrical resistance. It is named after the German scientist Georg Ohm, who studied the links between current, resistance and voltage in the 1820s.

Phonograph: The machine for recording and playing back sounds, invented by Edison in 1877, and later developed into the (disc-playing) gramophone.

Resistance: The degree to which a substance impedes the flow of an electric current.

Semaphore: A line-of-sight system of communication, in which coded signals are sent either by mechanical apparatus or by holding flags (or the arms) in different positions. It was invented in the 1790s.

Telegraph: A long-distance communications system (and its apparatus) involving the transmission of electrical signals in *Morse code* along wires connecting sender and receiver. It was developed over the 1830s and 1840s and is sometimes called "electric" to distinguish it from the earlier *semaphore* apparatus, which was also called the *telegraph*.

Volt: The unit, named after Alessandro Volta, used to measure electrical force or the degree of pressure "pushing" an electric current around a circuit.

THE LIBRARY
HAMLETS COLLEGE
HIGH STREET
LONDON E14 0AF
Tel: 071-538 5888

Index

American Civil War 15
  Battle of Shiloh 16, 19
Ampere 44, **63**

Batchelor, Charles 27, 32,
  33, 37, 39
Bell, Alexander Graham
  produces phonograph 51
  and telephone 7, 28, 29,
  31

Davy, Sir Humphry 42

Edison-effect lamp 60, **63**
Edison, Mary (née Stilwell)
  27, 51
Edison, Mina (née Miller)
  51
Edison, Thomas Alva
  birth 11
  childhood 11-15
  death 57
  and development of
    automobile 54-7
  develops electric light
    bulb 37-41
  develops electric power
    system 42-3, 47-9
  develops electric train 47
  develops kinetoscope
    52-3
  develops "Mary Ann"
    dynamo 45
  develops phonograph
    5-7, 34-7, 51-2
  early interest in science
    14-15
  and Edison-effect lamp
    60, **63**
  friendship with Henry
    Ford 54-6
  improves stock ticker 24
  and improvements to
    telephone 28-33
  inventions and projects
    7-9, 24-5, 54, 58-60
  legacy 58-60
  marriages 27, 51
  moves to Menlo Park 27-8
  newsboy on railway 15-17,
    20
  patent applications 24,
    53, 58
  sets up Newark factory 27
  and Western Union 23,
    26, 28, 33

"Wizard of Menlo Park"
  37
works as telegraph
  operator 20-2
Electromagnet 17, 19, 29, **63**
  Faraday's discovery of 29

Faraday, Michael 23, 29
  discovers the
    electromagnet 29
Fleming, Ambrose 60
Ford, Henry 55, 56, 57
  produces Model-T 56

Kinetoscope 52-3, **63**
Kreusi, John 5, 27, 36

Long-distance writer *see*
  telegraph, electric
"Long-waisted Mary Ann"
  44-7
Lumière brothers
  and kinetoscope 53

Menlo Park 28, 32, 37, 41,
  47, 50
Morse, Samuel 19
  invents code 19, **63**
Muybridge, Eadweard 52

Ohm, an 44, **63**
Ohm's Law 43-4

Phonograph 34-7, 50, 51-2,
  58, **63**
  Alexander Graham Bell
    and 51
  first recording made on
    5-7, 36

Resistance 30-1, 44, **63**

Sound-writer *see*
  phonograph
Stock ticker 24
Swan, Joseph 8

Telegraph, electric 16-19, **63**
Telephone, the
  Alexander Graham Bell
    and 28-30
  Edison's improvements to
    30-3

THE LEARNING CENTRE
TOWER HAMLETS COLLEGE
POPLAR CENTRE
POPLAR HIGH STREET
LONDON E14 0AF
Tel: 0171 538 5888